The Roman Colosseum

 GREAT STRUCTURES IN HISTORY

Other titles in the Great Structures in History
series include:

The Great Wall of China
A Medieval Castle
The Panama Canal
Stonehenge

The Roman Colosseum

GREAT STRUCTURES IN HISTORY

Lynn Kuntz

KIDHAVEN PRESS
An imprint of Thomson Gale, a part of The Thomson Corporation

Detroit • New York • San Francisco • San Diego • New Haven, Conn.
Waterville, Maine • London • Munich

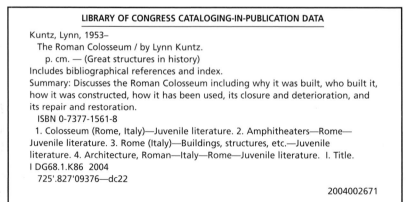

LIBRARY OF CONGRESS CATALOGING-IN-PUBLICATION DATA

Kuntz, Lynn, 1953–
    The Roman Colosseum / by Lynn Kuntz.
      p. cm. — (Great structures in history)
Includes bibliographical references and index.
Summary: Discusses the Roman Colosseum including why it was built, who built it, how it was constructed, how it has been used, its closure and deterioration, and its repair and restoration.
  ISBN 0-7377-1561-8
    1. Colosseum (Rome, Italy)—Juvenile literature. 2. Amphitheaters—Rome—Juvenile literature. 3. Rome (Italy)—Buildings, structures, etc.—Juvenile literature. 4. Architecture, Roman—Italy—Rome—Juvenile literature. I. Title.
I DG68.1.K86 2004
    725'.827'09376—dc22

                                                                2004002671

Printed in the United States of America

CONTENTS

CHAPTER ONE

The Magnificent Colosseum

The majestic Colosseum in Rome, Italy, is one of the most famous ruins in the world. Since the day it was completed in A.D. 80, it has been considered one of the most magnificent structures ever built by human hands. It is famous as a symbol of the incredible power and wealth of the Roman Empire. Because it is admired worldwide as an engineering and architectural masterpiece, the ideas used in its construction have been copied all over the globe. It is equally well-known for the violent, bloodthirsty games and countless cruel deaths that took place there.

Two thousand years ago the Roman Empire was the largest and most powerful **civilization** in the world. The Roman army conquered and controlled lands on three continents that are now part of thirty modern countries. The Romans were the most skilled builders of the ancient world. They used the riches they brought back from conquered lands to build spectacular buildings as monuments to their greatness.

Archaeologists—scientists who study the monuments, art, tools, and possessions of past human life—have been exploring the ruins of the Roman Empire for more than two hundred years. Thanks to their discoveries, and the fact that a large portion of the Colosseum remains standing, the modern world has a detailed picture of what the Colosseum was like in the glory days of the empire.

The Colosseum was an **amphitheater**. The word *amphitheater* comes from a Greek word meaning "all-around theater." An amphitheater is an oval-shaped stadium, with row upon row of seats rising above and

Although the Colosseum in Rome was completed in A.D. 80, it was designed and built so well that a large portion of it is still standing.

circling an open-air **arena**. Many modern sports stadiums are amphitheaters. The Colosseum was more than 600 feet (180 meters) long, 500 feet (150 meters) wide, and 160 feet (48 meters) tall. It was the size of sixty-four school buses parked bumper to bumper in a giant oval, with buses stacked on top of them to a height equal to a modern ten- or twelve-story building. The arena was the size of a football field.

This watercolor painting shows the oval-shaped amphitheater surrounding the open-air arena. Fifty thousand people could sit in the tiers of seats circling the arena, and the view was excellent from every seat.

Spectacularly Beautiful

The wealthy Roman emperor Vespasian, who had the Colosseum built, wanted it to amaze and awe everyone who saw it. A broad walkway of gleaming white **travertine**, a stone the Romans used in sculptures and fine buildings, led all the way around the Colosseum. The outside of the building appeared open and airy. Three levels, or very tall stories, were formed almost entirely of a series of graceful arches, called a **colonnade**. Eighty stone arches, each more than 20 feet (6 meters) tall and almost 14 feet (4.2 meters) wide, marched all the way around the building on each level. There were a total of 240 arches. The arches were separated from each other by strong, stately stone columns. The columns were of a special and distinct design for each level and lined up exactly with those in the level above.

Elegant statues filled some of the arches. Above the three levels of arches rose another level. Its outer wall was solid stone with large, rectangular windows. Glistening metal shields, heavy pieces of armor that warriors carried on one arm to protect themselves in battle, decorated the walls between the windows. All the outer walls, arches, and columns were covered with a layer of golden white, polished marble that appeared to glow when the sun shone on it at certain times of day.

Inside the Colosseum, many of the ceilings were painted purple and gold. Bubbling fountains with scented water sent a sweet, tangy mist into the air. Most of the walls were plastered, then painted white and red. Large wall paintings, called **frescoes**, splashed vibrant colors across some of the inside walls. Fancy borders of sculpted plaster, called **friezes**, trimmed many of the doorways. Tall statues decorated the hallways.

Cleverly Planned

The Colosseum's design allowed for many people to enter and exit the building quickly. There was a richly painted and sculpted entrance just for the emperor. A separate, but similar, entrance was built for other important leaders such as senators, priests and priestesses, and visiting royalty. There were seventy-six arched entrances for regular citizens.

Once a visitor to the Colosseum was inside, he or she could take one of four corridors that led all the way around the inside of the building. Seventy-two staircases led from the corridors to the different sections of the seating area, which was called the *cavea*. Spectators had tickets and assigned seats. Each ticket had a number on it that matched one of the entrance arches, which all had numbers above them. The ticket also listed a level and a seat number. The design was so clever that fifty thousand hurrying spectators could enter, show their tickets, and be seated in fifteen minutes.

Who got to sit where depended on how wealthy and important a person was. The best seats were nearest to the arena. A wall, called a **podium**, separated the arena from the *cavea*. The wall was wide and also served as a platform for the very finest seats in the Colosseum. The emperor sat in a luxurious box there. It was saved just for him and his guests. Other important people sat on

The main north entrance has been reconstructed to show the
beautiful frescoes and friezes that decorated the doors and walls
of the Colosseum.

the podium in marble seats that were covered with comfortable, colorful cushions. Each senator's name was carved in the marble base of his reserved seat. A low wall, gleaming with precious stones, separated the podium from the *cavea*, where ordinary Romans sat.

A fence was stretched all around the outside of the arena in front of the podium. Rollers were added to the top of the fence to make it impossible for even the most determined man or beast, both of which fought in the arena, to climb. High nets with spikes at the top hung alongside the fence to provide an extra layer of defense.

The Velarium

Behind the podium, the *cavea* slanted all the way up to the top of the Colosseum. Aisles divided the sixty or seventy rows of seats into wedge-shaped sections. Because the *cavea* angled steeply above the arena, the view was excellent from every seat. The poor, slaves, and foreigners stood at the very top.

Clever Roman architects even had plans for dealing with the weather. The arches and the windows let in refreshing breezes. The Colosseum had no roof, but giant canvas coverings, called the velarium, were rigged to provide comfortable shade for spectators. These awnings were supported by 240 wooden posts mounted in stone postholes on the top of the outer wall. Specially trained sailors from Rome's navy arranged and rearranged the velarium, using a system of ropes and pulleys, as the sun moved across the sky. If the emperor became displeased with a particular group of spectators, he could order the sailors to roll a certain section of the roof back. The burning sun would beat down on that unlucky, sweaty group, while everyone else in the Colosseum stayed cool under cover.

The Dark Side of the Colosseum

Beyond the beautiful **architecture** and smart design lay the dark and ugly heart of the Colosseum, the reason for its existence. Dozens of narrow, dimly lit passageways and damp, dirty cages for both wild beasts and humans were hidden from view beneath the wooden floor of the arena. There, wild beasts and **gladiators**, most of them slaves or prisoners condemned to die, were pushed and

A watercolor cutaway shows the dark passageways under the arena floor where wild animals and gladiators were kept in dirty, damp cages before being brought into the arena to kill or be killed.

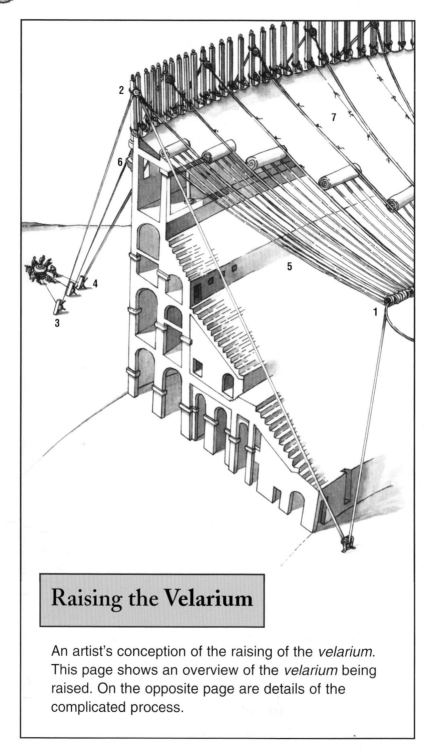

Raising the Velarium

An artist's conception of the raising of the *velarium*. This page shows an overview of the *velarium* being raised. On the opposite page are details of the complicated process.

A ring in the center of the amphitheater (1, at left) is raised by ropes running from the ring to pulleys on the top level (2) to stone blocks outside (3). Workers turn winches with pulleys (4) on these blocks, raising the ring. A second series of ropes runs from the underside of the rings (5) to pulleys and winches on the top gallery (6). The strips of the velarium (7) are unrolled onto this lower network of ropes, completing the awning.

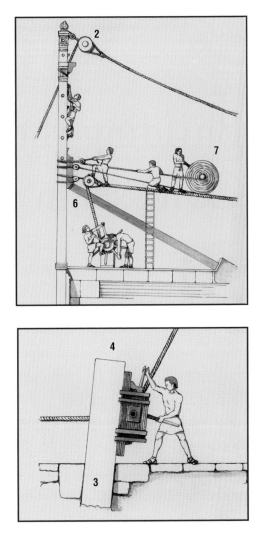

prodded through gates, along passages, up ramps, and through trapdoors into thirty-two elevator cages. The elevators, operated by weights, counterweights, ropes, and pulleys, lifted them into the arena. Suddenly they would be surrounded by the bright light of day and the screaming voices of thousands of spectators. Frightened and desperate, hearts pounding, they would have only two choices—to kill or be killed.

CHAPTER TWO

Building the Colosseum

Building the Colosseum was an enormous and ambitious task. Rome's greatest architects, the skilled professionals who decided how Rome's buildings and monuments should be built, designed the Colosseum. Four different contractors, the men in charge of planning and supervising the actual construction, worked side by side. Each was responsible for one quadrant, or quarter, of the building. The architects and contractors paid close attention to every detail, as shown by the near perfection of every part of the finished Colosseum.

The Foundation

The first task was to smooth out the ground of the building site to make it perfectly flat and level. This step was extremely important because the foundation would have to support millions of tons of stone, as well as the weight of tens of thousands of spectators. If the foundation was even slightly slanted, the weight would not be spread evenly. This would cause the building to crack and eventually collapse.

Roman surveyors were experts at measuring the land where a building was to be built. They used a tool called a *chorobates* to make sure the ground and foundation were level. A *chorobates* looked much like a long wooden bench. A horizontal crosspiece ran from one end piece to the other. Near each end a diagonal piece connected the horizontal crosspiece and the end piece. Perfectly straight, vertical lines were drawn, or carved, into the crosspiece, above each diagonal piece. Lines were also drawn on the diagonal pieces, directly below the lines on the crosspieces. A string with a metal weight on the end, called a plumb bob, was attached to the top of the crosspiece above the straight line. When it hung down, it hung in front of the line on the

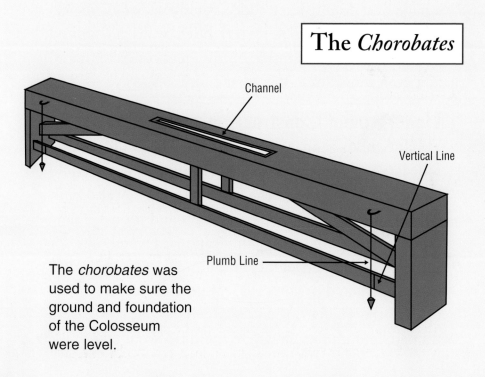

The *Chorobates*

Channel

Vertical Line

Plumb Line

The *chorobates* was used to make sure the ground and foundation of the Colosseum were level.

horizontal piece. The weight made each string hang straight down. If the weighted plumb strings lined up exactly with the lines on the horizontal crosspiece and the lines on the diagonal piece below, then the *chorobates* was exactly level. This meant the ground or foundation was exactly level.

In addition to being level and straight, the foundation had to be very strong. The Romans invented concrete, a mixture of fine volcanic ash, lime, and water, plus gravel or sand. This mix was like thick mud when wet, so it could be poured into the exact size and shape the builders wanted. When it dried, it was as hard as a rock. The builders of the Colosseum poured a 42-foot-deep (12.6 meter—about four underground stories) and 170-foot-wide (51 meter) concrete slab in the shape of a huge oval donut. They added 9-foot-wide (2.7 meter) and 18-foot-deep (5.4 meter) brick walls all around both the outside and inside of this great concrete ring to add even more strength and stability.

Underground Construction

While working on the foundation, the builders dug four large drains and a system of pipes so water could be moved in and out of the Colosseum. They also built dozens of underground passageways and rooms. There was an armory for storage of weapons, a warehouse for supplies, a first aid clinic, and animal cages. Builders also constructed prison cells, eating and sleeping quarters for the gladiators, a school where gladiators were trained, and a morgue where the dead were taken.

A Variety of Materials

After the foundation was complete the builders turned their attention to the framework of the building. They used a carefully chosen combination of materials to make the Colosseum extra strong. The various materials had different qualities: Some were lightweight, some were flexible, some were especially sturdy, and some were easy to shape and install. Huge blocks of travertine, which was known to withstand great pressure, were stacked four stories high and attached to each other with 300 tons (270,000 kilos) of iron clamps. These sturdy vertical supports were called piers. The piers were arranged

The underground piers were made from huge travertine blocks which came from a quarry twenty-five miles outside of Rome. These vertical supports could withstand great pressure and bore the weight of the massive building.

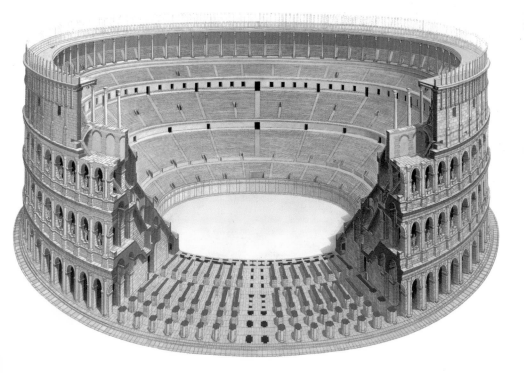

in rings, with one ring of piers encircled by another, and another. Then horizontal supports were added, attaching the piers to each other. Finally the walls were added.

The Romans built with two types of walls, each of which had two layers. One type had an inner layer of concrete with an outer layer of bricks. The other type

Statues were placed in many of the arches that went all around the building on three levels. Besides being decorative, the arches were able to support the weight of the huge building by distributing the downward pressure sideways.

was made of tufa, a lightweight stone Romans made by cementing volcanic ash with an outer layer of travertine. A final, decorative layer of tiles was made from clay mixed with water, sand, and straw. These tiles were added to many of the floors and walls.

Arches, Columns, and Vaults

The Romans used many arches, columns, and vaults in their important buildings, from temples to bridges to amphitheaters. Arches were built atop two piers of stone. Wedge-shaped stones were stacked to curve up and inward from the two piers. They joined in the middle, halfway between the two piers, in a keystone. In the Colosseum, 240 arches of the outer wall's colonnade were able to support the incredible weight of the huge building by distributing the downward pressure sideways. Arches were also used above almost every doorway. Columns were added for additional support.

Another major element of Roman architecture was the vault. A vault is a domed or curved ceiling. Vaulted ceilings made of concrete were used in almost all the passageways that led to the Colosseum's seating areas. Again, columns were used for additional support.

Workers and Tools

Hundreds of workers, including specially trained masons, blacksmiths, painters, carpenters, craftsmen, sculptors, and artists, worked on the Colosseum. Support teams of slaves fed the workers, hauled water for them to drink, and cleaned up human waste. Slaves also did much of the hard, backbreaking labor, like hauling and lifting. Slaves were used to build a road just for the purpose of hauling travertine from a quarry twenty-five miles (forty kilometers) away.

Scaffolding, a tall framework for workers to stand on, was built so that laborers could build tall walls. The scaffolding had to be sturdy enough to support the workers and their heavy tools. Cranes were used to lift supplies to higher levels. One type of crane consisted of a large round cage with a treadmill. Slaves turned the treadmill in order to hoist the cage, filled with heavy equipment and building materials, to the upper levels of construction.

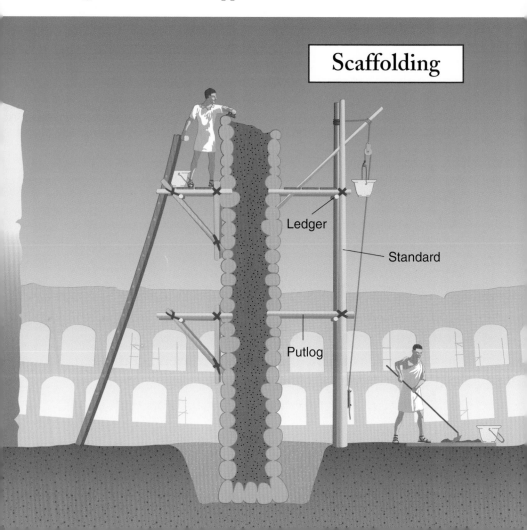

Scaffolding

Ledger

Standard

Putlog

Most Roman tools were made from iron and some had wooden handles. The stonemason's square and the axes the Romans used were similar in shape to modern tools. They used metal chisels hammered by wooden mallets to crack and split stone and a sharp metal tool, called a point, to carve stone. They used augers, drills tipped with metal and turned by hand, to drill into stone.

Finally, in A.D. 80, after eight long years of difficult and challenging labor, the Colosseum was completed. No one knows how much it cost in terms of dollars. But it is certain that the price was enormous. The cost in human suffering is even more difficult to calculate. Wars were fought and many lives lost as Rome took what belonged to others to pay for the building of the Colosseum.

CHAPTER THREE

A Day at the Colosseum

When the Colosseum was completed the citizens of Rome celebrated with a hundred-day festival of games that included animal acts, wild animal fights, hunts, and gladiatorial contests. Thereafter, the games often took place during Roman holidays that involved many days of feasting and partying. All over Rome huge billboards were painted on the sides of buildings advertising events at the Colosseum. On game days spectators began streaming into the Colosseum at sunrise. Many of them wore togas, the white robes worn by Roman citizens. The surrounding streets bustled with vendors selling food and wine and merchants peddling an assortment of wares in awning-covered stalls. Bets were placed and programs were bought.

Games from Dawn Until Dusk

Early in the day there were animal acts, much like those seen in a circus today. Monkeys, bears, goats, elephants, lions, and other exotic, trained animals performed a wide variety of tricks that amazed and thrilled the audience.

Next came wild animal fights. Various combinations of vicious animals were herded into the arena. When the animals were put together, their instincts compelled them to fight each other. At times several hundred animals roared and raged in the arena at once. When the crowds grew bored with the suffering of the bloodied, exhausted creatures, archers would shoot the animals.

Another type of animal fight involved armed human hunters stalking wild animals. In the opening games alone, between five thousand and nine thousand animals died. These included elephants, bears, lions, ostriches, panthers, rhinos, hippos, leopards, and crocodiles. As the

Spectators began arriving at the Colosseum at sunrise on game days. Trained elephants, monkeys, and other animals entertained the waiting audience during the morning.

years went on, such cruel carelessness for animal life caused several entire species to disappear from the Roman colonies in Africa and the Middle East.

Sometimes convicted criminals and (most researchers believe) Christians who refused to worship the gods of the emperor were thrown into the arena to be eaten alive by wild animals. On other occasions the arena was flooded and a naumachia, or sea battle, was fought between two ships full of slaves from captured enemy armies. The naumachia might go on until one or both armies were destroyed.

Mock battles on both land and water often included theatrical props—a large, artificial forest, for example, or a fort built on a small island in the center of an artificial lake. Various special effects could be achieved because certain sections of the arena floor could be lowered into large underground rooms beneath the arena. There they

A Roman mosaic illustrates some of the wild animal fights that took place before the gladiators came into the arena.

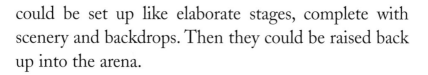

could be set up like elaborate stages, complete with scenery and backdrops. Then they could be raised back up into the arena.

Gladiator Fights

Afternoon fights between gladiators were favorite events. As the Roman Empire grew, warriors from conquered lands were marched back to Rome and sold as slaves. The biggest and strongest were bought and trained as gladiators at special *ludus* schools. Then they were made to fight other gladiators for the public's entertainment. Many criminals also were forced to become gladiators.

As the games became more and more popular, some free men even became gladiators, in hopes of gaining the favor of wealthy and important noblemen. If a gladiator survived many fights, he became a hero with the people, and the ruling emperor would pay him well to continue fighting. If he were a slave, he might even be freed. Eventually almost half of the gladiators were free men who liked the money, excitement, and glory of the successful fighting life. Occasionally women fought, too.

Gladiator Fight Rituals

The gladiatorial games began with a trumpet salute. This was followed by a grand parade, called the *pompa*, in which gladiators marched into the arena, carrying helmets that gleamed in the sun. Once in the arena, the gladiators raised their weapons to the emperor, or the highest nobleman present, and cried out, all together, "We who are about to die salute you!"

The Ludus Magnus was a gladiator school and barracks just outside the Colosseum (seen at the top of this painting). The biggest and strongest criminals or warriors from conquered lands were trained as gladiators here.

The weapons were then inspected to make sure they had been carefully sharpened. Many of the gladiators from conquered lands fought with the weapons they had been captured with, in the style of their home countries.

Styles of Gladiators

A Samnite was the most heavily armed gladiator. He wore leather and metal bands to protect his arms and left leg. He also wore a visored helmet with a high crest decorated with feathers, and a large, rectangular shield. He fought with a straight sword called a *gladius,* from which the word *gladiator* came. He was well protected, but his heavy armor made him slow and awkward.

A Retiarius warrior was almost naked. He wore no helmet. His only protection was a left arm guard with a large, flat shoulder piece. He was lightly armed, carrying only a weighted net, a fisherman's long spear with three prongs, and a short sword. His fighting strategy was to catch the other fighter in the net and then pierce him, the way a fisherman pierces his catch.

The Secutor, or chaser, got his name from his fighting method, which was to chase his opponent around the arena. The Secutor wore an oval-shaped helmet, especially designed so it could not be snagged in a net, with small, round eyeholes. He protected his left side by carrying a large shield in his left hand and wearing a metal guard on his left leg. He held a short, daggerlike sword.

A Thracian wore a crested helmet and thigh-high guards on both legs. He held a short sword called a *sica*

Four styles of gladiator are shown in this mosaic. The Samnite carried a rectangular shield; the Retiarius was almost naked; the Secutor wore an oval-shaped helmet; and the Thracian wore a crested helmet.

and carried a small, round shield called a *parma*. These were the weapons used by warriors in Thrace, an area of northern Greece. Other gladiators used looped ropes called lassos, or rode on horses and in chariots. Some of them had to fight blind, forced to wear helmets with no eyeholes.

Fights to the Death

Usually gladiators of two different types fought each other in the arena. The floor of the arena was built of wood and covered with sand. The sand could quickly soak up blood and be easily raked and smoothed over after a fight. Crowds were bloodthirsty and excitable, loudly booing the losers and cheering the winners. The more savage the struggle, the better the spectators liked it. Fights usually ended with the death of one of the gladiators.

If a gladiator had put up a great fight before being seriously injured, however, a referee would stop the fight. The injured gladiator might then be allowed to beg for his life. If the crowd demanded mercy from the emperor, the wounded man's life would be spared. If they demanded death, he would be killed on the spot. When a gladiator was killed, the dead body was dragged to the underground morgue.

Usually two different types of gladiators fought each other. In this painting, the Retiarius warrior has lost his net and has been injured by the Secutor's short sword.

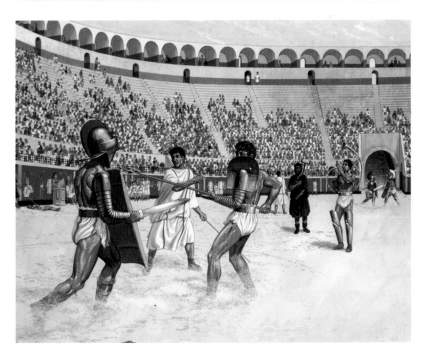

Games Abandoned

The games were wildly popular during the first century of the Colosseum's use. However, that began to change as Christianity became widely accepted throughout the empire. Rome's leaders began to view gladiator and animal fights as wrong. The public lost its taste for such bold brutality and bloodshed. Over the next few centuries the Roman army grew weaker. Rome was invaded and looted. It was no longer a rich city. Its citizens could not afford to keep the Colosseum in good condition, nor pay for the games.

When the last Roman emperor fell from power in A.D. 476, gladiator games had already been abolished. Animal events soon ended as well. After four and one-half centuries of showcasing the destruction and death of some for the pleasure of others, the Colosseum was shut down.

CHAPTER FOUR

The Colosseum Today

In the fifteen hundred plus years since the games stopped, the Colosseum has endured enormous challenge and change. For a thousand years after its massive doors were closed to spectators, it was ignored, neglected, and allowed to crumble into ruin. Powerful earthquakes, lightning strikes, and floods destroyed much of the structure. The vaulted ceilings collapsed, stucco and paint crumbled into dust, and wood rotted away. Thieves stole all of the valuable decorations, statues, and artwork. Thousands of wagonloads of beautiful marble were hauled away. The stone was used to mend city walls and bridges and to build churches, palaces, and a seaport.

Over the centuries the Colosseum was used as a fortress, a factory, a hideout for outlaws, a bullfighting ring, and even a garbage dump. Birds nested in its decaying bricks. Wild animals dug dens beneath the sagging walls and fallen stone. The arena was overgrown by a jungle of weeds and trees. Chambers and

The games and animal events at the Colosseum ended in the fifth century, and the building was neglected for a thousand years, as this eighteenth-century painting shows.

passageways beneath the arena caved in and filled with dirt. Most of the arches of the colonnade collapsed and were half buried in debris. The travertine was stained dark with age.

During all those years few Romans gave even a passing thought to the Colosseum's glorious past. That changed in the late eighteenth century when large numbers of travelers from various European countries began visiting Rome. By that time the once magnificent Colosseum was a frail, ghostly ruin, with less than half of the original structure remaining.

The north side of the outer wall, however, still stood proud and tall. So did almost the entire skeleton of that section of the structure. Thirty-one of the original eighty arches, the inner wall that supported the colonnade, and the encircling walls that had supported the *cavea* remained. It was more than enough to capture the attention and imagination of everyone who visited Rome. Famous artists began painting pictures of the

In the eighteenth century, interest in the Colosseum grew as travelers from other parts of Europe began to visit Rome. The Roman people decided to try to preserve what was left and to restore what could be repaired.

Colosseum, and popular writers wrote of it. Archaeologists began small-scale excavations, and plans were made to repair and protect the structure.

Repair and Restoration

By the early nineteenth century people from all over the educated world knew the history of the Colosseum and viewed it as a world treasure. Limited repairs were made off and on throughout that century. Support stones were added to weak sections. Arches that had been bricked over were uncovered, and some of the broken arches were rebuilt. The outer walls on the north side were reinforced with brick supports. Archaeologists began clearing rubble from underground chambers and passageways. Trees, bushes, and weeds that had overgrown the *cavea* and arena were removed.

Early in the twentieth century a small part of the *cavea*, including bench seating, was reconstructed. Constant small repairs were ongoing. But it was not until 1978 that a large-scale restoration of some of the arches was begun. Then, in the 1990s, an enormous, multimillion-dollar, years-long project was undertaken. The goal was to repair and stabilize every possible part of the Colosseum. Work began with extensive restoration and cleaning of the outer face of the travertine arches. As soon as this work was underway, a major restoration of the foundation began. Scaffolding was then built so that reconstruction of the outer walls could begin.

Work will likely not end with these efforts. Experts estimate that air pollution in the last fifty years has caused more damage to the stone of the Colosseum than almost

In the 1990s, after years of small repair projects, Romans began an enormous project to repair, rebuild, stabilize, and restore as much of the Colosseum as possible.

two thousand years of wind and rain. A stream that runs beneath the Colosseum and the vibrations of a nearby subway pose ongoing threats to the structure's stability. In 2003 more than 2.5 million tourists visited the Colosseum. Such human traffic is sure to further wear away the marble floors and stairways. Repairs and rebuilding will probably be necessary far into the future.

Buried Secrets

Even though less than half the structure remains, the Colosseum is complete enough to give archaeologists and historians an excellent idea of life in Rome two thousand years ago. Artifacts found in the ruins include an ancient lamp in the shape of a gladiator's helmet. A stone carving shows trumpeters and the parade that opened the games. A terra-cotta sculpture features the *bestiarrii*, or animal slayers, battling wild lions and bears. Bronze statues and figurines of many types of gladiators,

Archaeologists have uncovered many artifacts like these clay gladiators at the Colosseum site. These discoveries give an excellent idea of what happened at the games and gladiator fights almost two thousand years ago.

dressed in battle costume and displaying distinctive weapons, have been unearthed. Coins bearing the image of the Colosseum show not only the outer walls, but a glimpse into the interior.

Archaeologists have also learned a lot about Roman building methods as various tools and pieces of equipment used in the construction of the Colosseum have been discovered. Researchers have been able to piece together still more information by interpreting signs in the stone. For example, little holes in the Colosseum walls indicate where scaffolding was attached to the travertine building blocks.

Many Mysteries Remain

There is much, however, still to learn. For instance, archaeologists discovered a series of man-sized cubicles built into stone walls near the arena. No one yet knows what they were for. Some think guards with bows and arrows might have been stationed there, ready to shoot any animal or human that tried to escape the arena. Others think these spaces might have been for toilets. A new set of questions was recently raised by the discovery of a drawing on a second-story corridor. Historians wonder who drew the crouching gladiator armed with a bow and arrow—and why. Some believe a spectator did it, probably a teenage boy or an adult man, since the drawing is in a place too high for a child to reach. Possibly he was bored, waiting for the fights to begin. These are just two, among many, of the Colosseum's mysteries that archaeologists have yet to solve.

In 2003 more than 2.5 million people from all over the world visited the Colosseum, making it Italy's most popular tourist attraction.

One of the World's Most Visited Sites

So many visitors from all over the world come to Rome each year to visit the Colosseum that it has become Italy's most popular tourist attraction by far. People come for many reasons. Those fascinated by Roman history want to see the ultimate symbol of the empire's greatness. Artists and engineers want to marvel at the architecture. Sports fans want to see the design that inspired modern stadiums and arenas. Some want to see the setting that has been re-created in many works of art and literature. Others come to pay tribute to many thousands who died there. Almost everyone wonders at how so beautiful a building could have been used for such an ugly purpose.

The rumble of footsteps in the Colosseum now comes from foreign tourists, rather than Roman spectators. The voices heard are those of enthusiastic tour guides speaking in many languages, rather than the Latin shouts of an excitable crowd. The roars of wild animals have been replaced by the calls of birds and the occasional howls of the many stray cats that live in the Colosseum. Still, when modern-day visitors sit, still and quiet, in the reconstructed *cavea*, they can quite easily imagine the Colosseum in its gory glory days.

Glossary

A.D.: An abbreviation for the Latin words *anno Domini*, which mean "in the year of our Lord." Used to measure time, beginning with the number of years since the accepted date of Christ's birth.

amphitheater: A large, oval-shaped stadium where thousands of spectators sit in circular rows of seats, surrounding an open space, and watch public entertainment.

architecture: The art of planning, designing, and building structures.

arena: The open-air, sand-covered floor in the center of Roman amphitheaters where gladiators and animals fought.

cavea: The main seating section in the Roman Colosseum.

civilization: An organized society with social customs, a government structure, and artistic tradition.

colonnade: A series of evenly spaced columns that usually support the upper story or roof of a building.

fresco: A painting made with watercolors on wet plaster.

frieze: A strip of painting or carving that often tells a story.

gladiator: A professional fighter in the Roman Empire who fought other gladiators to the death, for the entertainment of spectators.

podium: The seating area closest to the arena in an amphitheater, reserved for men from the highest level of Roman society.

scaffolding: A framework, usually wooden. Built against the walls of a building under construction for workers to stand on.

travertine: A tough, sturdy, creamy white limestone commonly used in ancient Roman building.

For Further Reading

Books

Joanne Jessop, *The X-Ray Picture Book of Big Buildings of the Ancient World.* Danbury, CT: Franklin Watts, 1993. Provides an overview of unique buildings of the ancient world, including the Roman Colosseum, and includes color diagrams and illustrations.

David Macaulay, *City, a Story of Roman Planning and Construction.* Boston: Houghton Mifflin, 1974. Text and black-and-white illustrations show how the Romans planned and built important structures during the empire years.

John Malam, *Gladiator: Life and Death in Ancient Rome.* New York: Dorling Kindersley, 2002. Covers everything from the rise of Rome, to the Colosseum's glory days, to the lives of everyday Romans. Also describes the lives and training of gladiators until the decline and fall of the empire. Lots of good illustrations.

Don Nardo, *Roman Amphitheaters.* New York: Franklin Watts, 2002. Describes the history and cultural importance of amphitheaters in the Roman Empire. Includes many color photographs and illustrations.

Richard Watkins, *Gladiator.* New York: Houghton Mifflin, 1997. Details the history of gladiators, including types of armor, use of animals, amphitheaters, and how gladiatorial fights fit into Roman society for almost seven hundred years.

Philip Wilkinson, *Amazing Buildings.* New York: Dorling Kindersley, 1993. Offers information about and color illustrations of famous buildings, including the Roman Colosseum.

Web Sites

The Colosseum: A Site on the Roman Amphitheater (www.the-colosseum.net). Created by Andrea Pepe, Daniele Pepe, and Catherine McElwee, this site provides details on many aspects of the Colosseum and includes an excellent picture gallery of color photos.

Dead Romans (www.deadromans.com). Created by Tim Ryan, this site has information about Roman life during the empire years, including close to two hundred photos of the Colosseum.

The Great Buildings Collection (www.greatbuildings. com). An architecture reference site, this is a gateway to architecture around the world and across history. Includes 3-D spatial models of the Colosseum, photos and plan drawings, commentaries, and Web links.

Roman Colosseum—Amphitheatrum Flavium (http:// ancienthistory.about.com). A great resource for information on the Roman Colosseum, with lots of links.

The Roman Colosseum at GladiatorSchool.tv (www. gladiatorschool.tv). Lots of details about the life of a gladiator, with great links.

Index

Picture Credits

About the Author

Lynn Kuntz is an award-winning writer whose nonfiction children's book credits include *The Naturalist's Handbook, Activities for Young Explorers*, and *American Grub, Eats for Kids from All Fifty States* (cowritten with Jan Fleming). Kuntz has written newspaper and magazine fiction and nonfiction, five award-winning films for children, and one feature family film, *Dakota*. Kuntz has received a number of awards, including the Press Club Award for Outstanding Achievement in Journalism and the Colorado Author's League Best Children's Book of the Year Award. She teaches writing for children in the Extended Studies Program at Fort Lewis College. Kuntz, the mother of four children, lives in Colorado and loves to ski, hike, and ride horses in the mountains.